Approved by LEO

The finest seal of approval based on taste, looks and durability. All done by my son Leo at 1,5 years old.

COPYRIGHTS

Publisher: Skyborn Works
Ilustrations: Simon Zingerman
Typography: Block Pro+, Knewave, FF Providence Sans and Interstate.
OFL: The font software Knewave is licensed under the SIL Open Font License, Version 1.1. Author: Tyler Finck, Copyright © 2010.

ISBN

ISBN-13: 978-91-980904-5-1

CONTACT INFO

Skyborn Works, Lyckselevagen 38, LGH 1102. 162 67 Vallingby. SWEDEN.
T: +46 73 649 83 11
contact@skybornworks.com

www.futurelittle.com
www.skybornworks.com

GYM BAG

FITNESS CLOTHING

ATHLETIC SHOES

WATER BOTTLE

WORKOUT MUSIC

FITNESS CENTER

MEMBERSHIP
CARD

PERSONAL TRAINER

WORKOUT ROUTINE

WEEKLY PLANNER

DAYS	PLAN
MONDAY	Arms/Back
TUESDAY	Cardio
WEDNESDAY	Abs/Core
THURSDAY	Yoga
FRIDAY	Full Body
SATURDAY	Legs
SUNDAY	REST!

EXERCISES

EXERCISE MACHINES

WEIGHT
BENCH

DUMBBELL & KETTLEBELL

BARBELLS

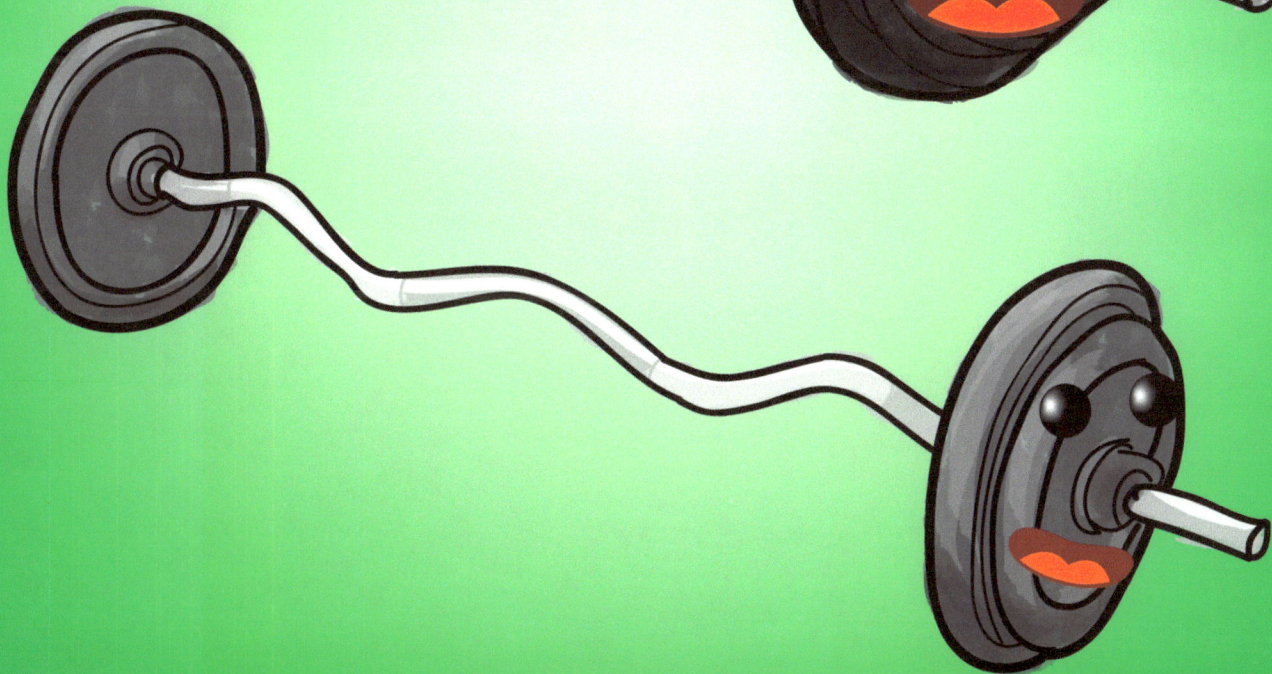

PUNCHING BAGS

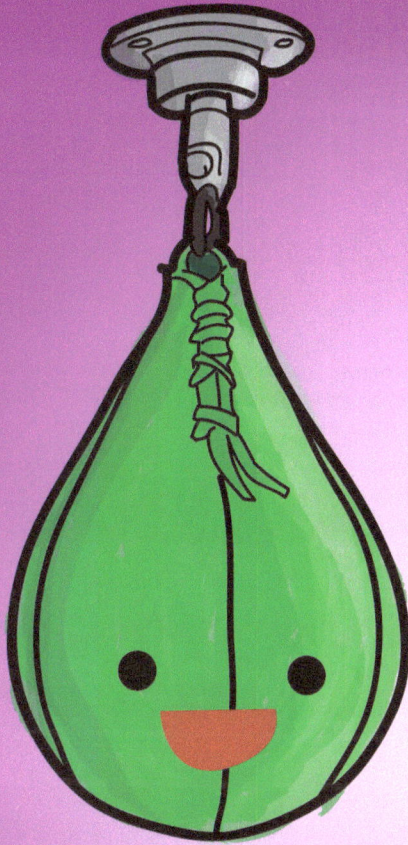

EXERCISE BALL

EXERCISE
MAT

SHAKER BOTTLE

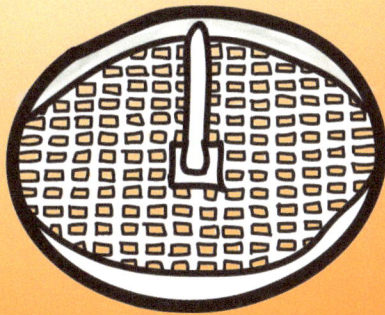

HEALTHY FOOD & DRINKS

OUTDOOR GEAR

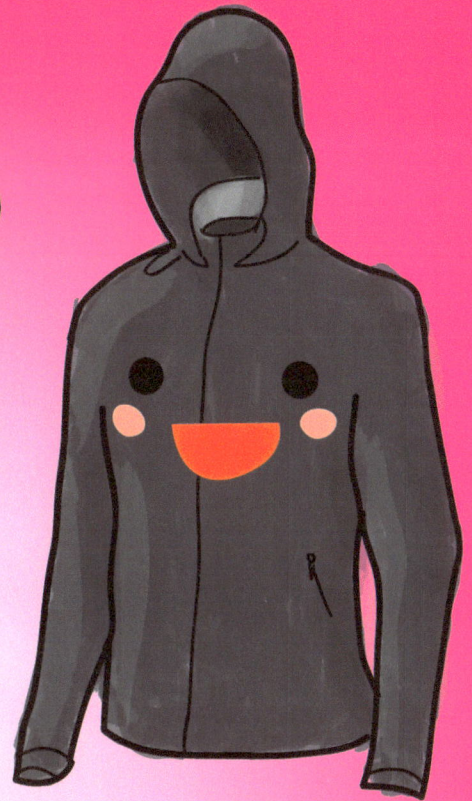

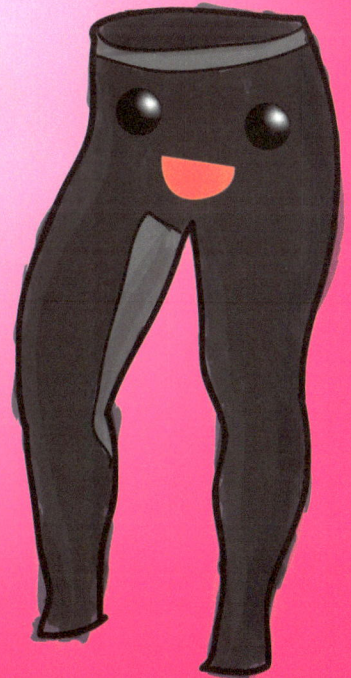

ACTIVITY TRACKER

FITNESS APPS

STEP ONE

RUNNING

APPLICATIONS

www.ingramcontent.com/pod-product-compliance
Lightning Source LLC
Chambersburg PA
CBHW042100040426

42448CB00002B/77